What Do You Know About
Atoms and Molecules ?

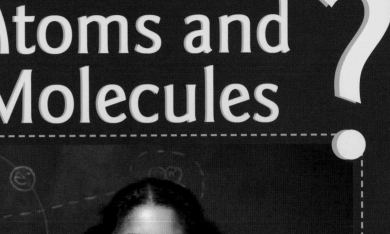

PowerKiDS
press

Tilda Monroe

New York

Published in 2011 by The Rosen Publishing Group, Inc.
29 East 21st Street, New York, NY 10010

First Edition

Editor: Amelie von Zumbusch
Book Design: Kate Laczynski
Layout Design: Ashley Burrell
Photo Researcher: Jessica Gerweck

Illustration Credits: pp. 8, 10 (left) Dorling Kindersley/Getty Images; p. 11 by Ginny Chu, adapted from an illustration by Tahara Anderson; p. 13 by Ashley Burrell, adapted from an illustration by Ginny Chu; pp. 14 (left), 15 by Ginny Chu. p. 17 (right) © www.iStockphoto.com/Henrik Jonsson; p. 19 (top) by Ben Mills (http://commons.wikimedia.org/wiki/File:Alpha-lactose-from-xtal-3D-balls.png).

Photo Credits: Cover Hill Street Studios/Getty Images; pp. 5, 16, 17 (left), 18, 19 (bottom) Shutterstock.com; p. 6 © www.iStockphoto.com/Bonnie Jacobs; p. 7 D. Sharon Pruitt Pink Sherbet Photography/Getty Images; p. 9 Clive Streeter/Getty Images; p. 10 (right) © www.iStockphoto.com/Roydee; p. 12 Jamie Grill/Getty Images; p. 14 (right) © www.iStockphoto.com/Dan Bachman; p. 20 (top) Time & Life Pictures/Getty Images; p. 20 (bottom) Getty Images; p. 21 Tipp Howell/Getty Images; p. 22 © www.iStockphoto.com/Hans F. Meir

Library of Congress Cataloging-in-Publication Data

Monroe, Tilda.
   What do you know about atoms and molecules? / Tilda Monroe. — 1st ed.
      p. cm. — (20 questions: physical science)
   Includes index.
   ISBN 978-1-4488-0669-0 (library binding) — ISBN 978-1-4488-1223-3 (pbk.) — ISBN 978-1-4488-1224-0 (6-pack)
   1. Atoms—Juvenile literature. 2. Molecules—Juvenile literature. I. Title.
   QC173.16.M66 2011
   539.7—dc22   2009052052

Manufactured in the United States of America

CPSIA Compliance Information: Batch #WS10PK: For Further Information contact Rosen Publishing, New York, New York at 1-800-237-9932

Contents

It's Physical!

You have likely studied science in school. You may have learned about animals or the water cycle. Do you know what physical science is, though? It is the study of matter and energy. Everything around you is made up of matter, from your body to your socks to the air you breathe. What is matter, though? Matter is anything made up of atoms and molecules.

Atoms and molecules are so tiny that you cannot see them. Yet if it were not for them, the world would not be here. That is a big thought about some really tiny things!

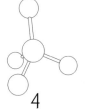

Anything you can touch is made of matter. Natural things, such as air and snow, are matter. Manmade things, such as gloves and boots, are matter, too.

1. What are atoms anyway?

You can think about atoms as the building blocks from which all matter is built. On their own, atoms might not seem like much. When a whole bunch of them get together, though, cool stuff happens. Atoms make up the water in all the world's oceans. They make up the stars in the sky. From diamonds to raindrops, everything is made of atoms!

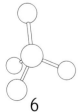

Have you ever looked at rocks through a magnifying glass? Rocks are made of atoms. They are too small to see, though, even with a magnifying glass. Magnifying glasses are made of atoms, too!

Even though atoms are tiny, they are made up of even smaller parts. There are three main kinds of parts. They are electrons, protons, and neutrons.

Atoms are very, very small. In fact, there are about 60 million million million atoms in one grain of sand!

Protons and neutrons are always in the center of an atom. Scientists call the center of an atom the nucleus. An atom can have more than one proton and neutron in its nucleus.

An electron is always busy because it never stops moving. An atom's electrons **orbit** the nucleus, just as planets orbit the Sun. There can be lots of electrons in an atom. All of them spin around the nucleus.

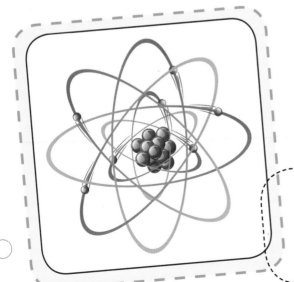

You can see the protons, neutrons, and electrons in this drawing of an atom. The protons and neutrons are together in the nucleus. The electrons are the blue balls spinning around the nucleus.

5. Does the number of parts in an atom matter?

Although all atoms have the same basic parts, they are not all the same. Atoms with different numbers of protons are different kinds of atoms. This difference makes one atom **hydrogen** and another iron.

The number of protons an atom has sets what kind of atom it is. Atoms of copper (left) have 29 protons. Zinc (right), on the other hand, has 30 protons in each atom.

Scientists have named more than 100 different elements, or kinds of atoms. Some well-known elements are silver, gold, and **oxygen**. Atoms of an element always have the same number of protons. For example, hydrogen has one proton. It also has one electron. Atoms generally have the same number of protons as electrons.

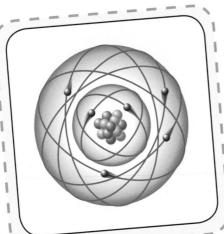

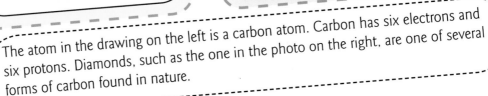

The atom in the drawing on the left is a carbon atom. Carbon has six electrons and six protons. Diamonds, such as the one in the photo on the right, are one of several forms of carbon found in nature.

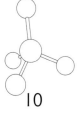

A chart called the periodic table lists all the known elements. It gives the names of the elements. It also lists each element by its **symbol**. Each element has a one, two, or three-letter symbol that stands for it. The chart also includes the element's atomic number. This tells you how many protons an element has.

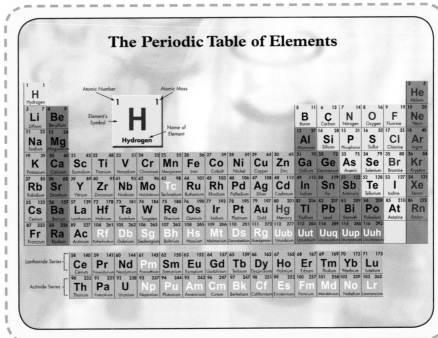

The Periodic Table of Elements

In the periodic table, elements are listed in the order of their atomic numbers. Each row going across is called a period. The rows going down are known as groups.

11

Electrons and protons have an **electric charge**. Electrons always have a negative charge, shown by a minus sign (-). Protons have a positive charge, shown with a plus sign (+). Neutrons are neutral. This means they have no charge at all. This neutral charge is shown with a zero (0).

Electricity happens because of the electric charges in atoms. We use electricity to power many things, such as electric lights.

9. Do atoms have an overall charge?

When atoms have the same number of protons and electrons, they are neutral. Atoms are not always balanced, though. Sometimes an atom loses an electron. Then, it carries a positive charge because it has more protons than electrons. If an atom gains an electron, it has a negative charge. Atoms that are not neutral are called ions.

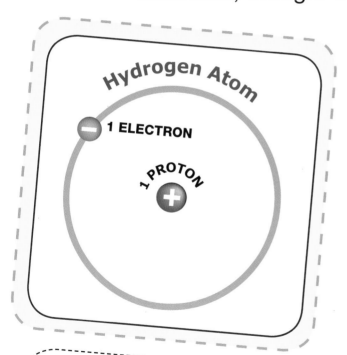

Hydrogen Atom

1 ELECTRON

1 PROTON

This drawing of a hydrogen atom shows the atom's positive proton and negative electron. Hydrogen atoms are the simplest atoms. They have one proton, one electron, and no neutrons.

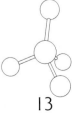

Yes, atoms can join together. They do this by forming bonds. Bonds form when two atoms share or borrow electrons from each other.

The salt (right) we put on our food is also called sodium chloride. The drawing on the left shows how a sodium atom gives up an electron to a chlorine atom to form sodium chloride. This forms an ionic bond between them.

11. What kinds of bonds are there?

The two main kinds of bonds are covalent and ionic bonds. Covalent bonds happen when two atoms share electrons. For example, when two hydrogen atoms become linked together, they form a covalent bond. An ionic bond forms when one atom gives up or takes an electron from another atom. This forms two ions with opposite charges. The ions stick together because they are attracted to each other like magnets.

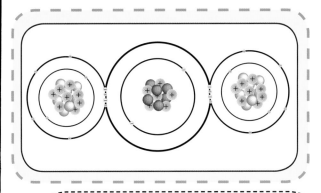

In carbon dioxide, two oxygen atoms form covalent bonds with a carbon atom. Carbon dioxide is a common gas. People produce it when we breathe out or burn things.

12. What are bonded atoms called?

Atoms that are bonded together are called molecules.

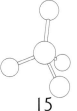

15

13. Are the atoms in molecules always the same?

Molecules can be made from atoms of the same element. They can also be made from different elements. For example, a molecule of oxygen gas is made up of two oxygen atoms. Oxygen is a gas that people must breathe to stay alive. On the other hand, a water molecule is made up of two hydrogen atoms and one oxygen atom.

People are not the only living things that need oxygen. All animals, including dogs, must have oxygen to live and grow.

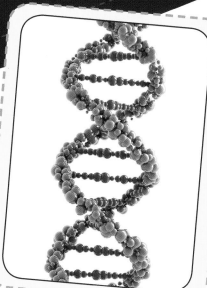

DNA (right) is a complex molecule. It controls how living things grow and what they look like. Sisters (left) look somewhat alike because their DNA molecules are nearly, but not quite, the same.

14. How many atoms are in a molecule?

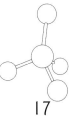

Some molecules, such as oxygen and water, are made up of just a few atoms. These are called simple molecules. There are also many **complex** molecules. These can have hundreds or thousands of atoms in one molecule.

Scientists use chemical formulas to talk about the atoms that make up molecules. For example, the formula for water is H_2O. This tells us that every water molecule has two hydrogen atoms and one oxygen atom.

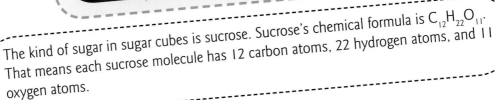

The kind of sugar in sugar cubes is sucrose. Sucrose's chemical formula is $C_{12}H_{22}O_{11}$. That means each sucrose molecule has 12 carbon atoms, 22 hydrogen atoms, and 11 oxygen atoms.

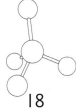

Milk (bottom) is a healthy drink. The sugar lactose is found in milk. This drawing of a lactose molecule (top) shows oxygen atoms in red, hydrogen atoms in white, and carbon atoms in black.

Some of the biggest, most complex molecules are found inside plants and animals. These molecules are called **organic compounds**. They all have the element carbon in them. Glucose is one example of an organic compound. It is a form of sugar. Its formula is $C_6H_{12}O_6$. This tells us that each glucose molecule has 6 carbon atoms, 12 hydrogen atoms, and 6 oxygen atoms.

17. When were atoms discovered?

The first person known to have talked about atoms is the Greek philosopher Democritus. He lived around 2,500 years ago. Democritus believed that everything in the world was made up of tiny pieces that were too small to see.

DEMOCRITVS.

Democritus was born around 460 BC. He wrote about many subjects, such as the natural world, math, and how people see.

In 1932, the English scientist James Chadwick, seen here, proved that neutrons existed.

18. Who discovered electrons and protons?

The English scientist J. J. Thomson discovered electrons in 1897. In 1918, Ernest Rutherford proved that atoms had protons.

For a long time, scientists did not have tools that let them see atoms. Today, scientists use **electron microscopes**. These tools let them learn about the shape, **structure**, and **properties** of atoms and molecules.

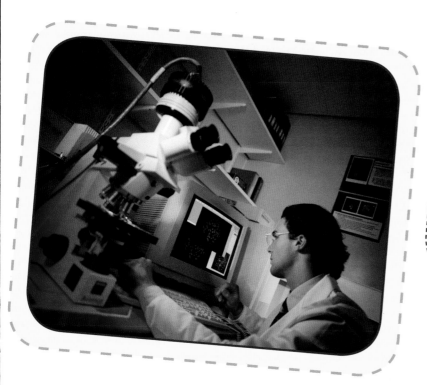

The first electron microscopes were made in the 1930s. Today, electron microscopes like the one on the left have become important tools for many scientists.

20. Why are atoms and molecules important?

Everything around us is made from atoms and molecules. Studying atoms and molecules gives scientists clues that help them understand our world.

Knowing the properties of matter lets **engineers** build bridges that reach across huge spaces. A whole branch of science, called **genetics**, has grown up around the study of the DNA molecule.

What will scientists discover about atoms and molecules in the years to come? There is still so much to learn.

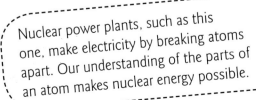

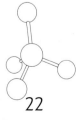

Nuclear power plants, such as this one, make electricity by breaking atoms apart. Our understanding of the parts of an atom makes nuclear energy possible.

Glossary

complex (kom-PLEKS) Having many parts.

electric charge (ih-LEK-trik CHAHRJ) Something some matter has that can produce power.

electron microscopes (ih-LEK-tron MY-kruh-skohps) Powerful tools used to see very tiny things.

engineers (en-juh-NEERZ) Masters at planning and building engines, machines, roads, and bridges.

genetics (jih-NEH-tiks) The study of how features are passed down from parents to children.

hydrogen (HY-dreh-jen) A colorless gas that weighs less than any other known kind of matter.

orbit (OR-bit) To travel in a circular path.

organic compounds (or-GA-nik KOM-powndz) Things that have molecules with carbon in them.

oxygen (OK-sih-jen) A gas that has no color or taste and is necessary for people and animals to breathe.

properties (PRAH-pur-teez) Features that belong to something.

structure (STRUK-cher) Form.

symbol (SIM-bul) The letter or letters that stand for an element.

Index

Web Sites

Due to the changing nature of Internet links, PowerKids Press has developed an online list of Web sites related to the subject of this book. This site is updated regularly. Please use this link to access the list:
www.powerkidslinks.com/quest/am/

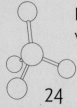